Singular und Plural

A. Bilde den Plural der folgenden Substantive.

books	Buch	plan	
planes	Flugzeug	minute	
answers	Antwort	apple	
faces	Gesicht	chair	
boxes	Schachtel	dress	
tables	Tisch	page	
sandwiches	Sandwich	pencil case	
bridges	Brücke	desk	
hours	Stunde	brush	
teachers	Lehrer	pupil	

B. Bei welchen der folgenden Substantive wird die Pluralendung wie /iz/ ausgesprochen? Unterstreiche diese Substantive.

pages	exercises	churches	clothes	houses
faces	roles	stages	theatres	buses
titles	languages	phrases	pieces	centres
bridges	cornflakes	messages	places	brochures
voices	noises	noses	horses	scenes
brushes	cakes	classes	glasses	tables

Lösung

A.

books	plans
planes	minutes
answers	apples
faces	chairs
boxes	dresses
tables	pages
sandwiches	pencil cases
bridges	desks
hours	brushes
teachers	pupils

B.

ages	bridges
exercises	cornflakes
churches	messages
clothes	places
houses	brochures
faces	voices
roles	noises
stages	noses
theatres	horses
buses	scenes
titles	brushes
languages	cakes
phrases	classes
pieces	glasses
centres	tables

Singular und Plural

A. Bilde den Singular der folgenden Substantive.

days	______	boys	______
babies	______	families	______
thieves	______	plays	______
wives	______	knives	______
shelves	______	countries	______
parties	______	lives	______
halves	______	hobbies	______

B. Wie lautet der Plural?

man	______	woman	______
child	______	tooth	______
foot	______	goose	______
mouse	______		

Lösung

A.

day
baby
thief
wife
shelf
party
half

boy
family
play
knife
country
life
hobby

B.

men
children
feet
mice
women
teeth
geese

s-Genitiv

A. Verbinde die Substantive mit dem *s*-Genitiv.

Tom/house ______________________

Mr Benson/car ______________________

Mr Benson/wife ______________________

the Bensons/hobbies ______________________

my parents/bikes ______________________

my sisters/friends ______________________

my mother/brother ______________________

my brother/CDs ______________________

Mr Mason/lessons ______________________

the pupils/workbooks ______________________

my grandparents/radio ______________________

B. Setze die markierten Substantive in den Plural und verbinde sie mit dem *s*-Genitiv.

the baby/toys ______________________

the girl/mother ______________________

the boy/shoes ______________________

my uncle/brothers ______________________

my cousin/teacher ______________________

my aunt/letters ______________________

Lösung

A. Tom's house
Mr Benson's car
Mr Benson's wife
the Bensons' hobbies
my parents' bikes
my sisters' friends
my mother's brother
my brother's CDs
Mr Mason's lessons
the pupils' workbooks
my grandparents' radio

B. the babies' toys
the girls' mother
the boys' shoes
my uncles' brothers
my cousins' teacher
my aunts' letters

Der unbestimmte Artikel

A. Setze *a/an* vor die folgenden Substantive.

______ name	_______ friend	_______ aunt
______ year	_______ invitation	_______ game
______ school	_______ example	_______ uncle
______ teacher	_______ song	_______ exercise
______ pupil	_______ unit	_______ pencil
______ number	_______ question	_______ ruler
______ uniform	_______ answer	_______ evening
______ eye	_______ island	_______ library

B. Setze den unbestimmten Artikel ein. Entscheide dich zwischen *a* oder *an*.

___ useful exercise	___ funny exercise	___ beautiful exercise
___ interesting exercise	___ long exercise	___ intelligent exercise
___ complicated exercise	___ short exercise	___ important exercise
___ difficult exercise	___ good exercise	___ bad exercise
___ easy exercise	___ German exercise	___ awful exercise
___ English exercise	___ terrible exercise	___ terrible exercise
___ boring exercise	___ silly exercise	___ old exercise

Lösung

A.

a name
a year
a school
a teacher
a pupil
a number
a uniform
an eye
a friend
an invitation
an example
a song
a unit
a question
an answer
an island
an aunt
a game
an uncle
an exercise
a pencil
a ruler
an evening
a library

B.

a useful exercise
an interesting exercise
a complicated exercise
a difficult exercise
an easy exercise
an English exercise
a boring exercise
a funny exercise
a long exercise
a short exercise
a good exercise
a German exercise
a terrible exercise
a silly exercise
a beautiful exercise
an intelligent exercise
an important exercise
a bad exercise
an awful exercise
an exciting exercise
an old exercise

Der Demonstrativbegleiter

A. Setze in den Plural.

this family ______________________

that boy ______________________

this man ______________________

that lady ______________________

this class ______________________

that page ______________________

this foot ______________________

this child ______________________

this policewoman ______________________

that adult ______________________

this house ______________________

B. Setze die entsprechenden Formen von *this* ein.

________ is a man and ________ are women.

________ is a child and ________ are children, too.

________ is a teacher and ________ are teachers, too.

________ is a mouse and ________ are mice, too.

________ is my friend and ________ are your friends.

Lösung

A.

these families
those boys
these men
those ladies
these classes
those pages

these feet
these children
these policewomen
those adults
these houses

B.

This is a man and these are women.
This is a child and these are children, too.
This is a teacher and these are teachers, too.
This is a mouse and these are mice, too.
This is my friend and these are your friends.

Der Possessivbegleiter

A. Setze die passenden Possessivbegleiter ein.

This is *my* friend. These are ______________ friends. (1. Person Plural)

This is *your* bike. These are ______________ bikes. (2. Person Plural)

This is *his* car. These are ______________ cars. (3. Person Plural)

This is *her* room. These are ______________ rooms. (3. Person Plural)

This is *its* bone. These are ______________ bones. (3. Person Plural)

B. Setze die richtigen Formen des Possessivbegleiters ein.

1. I've got a bike. This is _________ bike.
2. Sue has got a bike, too. That's ____________ bike.
3. Have you got a bike, Mrs Benson? Is that __________ bike over there?
4. The saddle of the bike is new. ____________ saddle is new.
5. The Bensons have got a car. That's _____________ car.
6. We have got a new English book. This is ___________ new book.

Lösung

A. our friends
your bikes
their cars
their rooms
their bones

B.
1 This is **my** bike.
2 That's **her** bike.
3 Is that **your** bike over there?
4 **Its** saddle is new.
5 That's **their** car.
6 This is **our** new book.

Zusammensetzungen mit *no, any, some*

A. Übersetze.

a **Nobody** likes him. ____________________

b He likes **nobody**. ____________________

c He does**n't** like **anyone**. ____________________

d He does**n't** like **anything**. ____________________

e He likes **nothing**. ____________________

f He goes **nowhere**. ____________________

g He does**n't** go **anywhere**. ____________________

h You wo**n't** see him **anywhere**. ____________________

i He does**n't** want to see **anything**. ____________________

B. Setze *jemand*, *etwas* etc. ein.

________________ must talk to him. (jemand)

We must do __________ about him. (etwas)

But what can we do? Can we really do __________ ? (etwas)

We must find some help ______________ . (irgendwo)

We must find ___________ to help him. (jemanden)

If we don't, __________ terrible will happen. (etwas)

Lösung

A.
- **a** niemand
- **b** niemanden
- **c** niemanden
- **d** nichts
- **e** nichts
- **f** nirgends
- **g** nirgends
- **h** nirgends
- **i** nichts

B.
Somebody/Someone must talk to him.
We must do something about him.
But what can we do? Can we really do anything?
We must find some help somewhere.
We must find somebody to help him.
If we don't, something terrible will happen.

Zeitangaben mit Präpositionen

A. Zeit- und Ortsangaben enthalten oft Präpositionen. Eine kleine Liste solcher Zeitangaben findest du hier. Setze die richtige Präposition ein.

________	the morning	________	my birthday
________	the evening	________	the morning of my birthday
________	the afternoon	________	February, 3rd
________	three o'clock	________	December
________	night	________	June
________	Christmas	________	2008
________	three o'clock (vor)	________	three o'clock (nach)
________	three o'clock (bis)	________	morning ________night

B. Ergänze die richtigen Präpositionen.

Tom was born ______ 1997.

His birthday is ______ April.

It is ______ April 2nd. His friend's birthday is ______ the same day.

It's __________ a Friday this year.

_______ Saturday they are going to have a big party.

It's always fun to have parties _______ the weekend!

It will begin _________ 3 o'clock and end _____ 11.

They'll prepare for the party ________ morning ________ night (von/bis) on Friday.

Lösung

A. in the morning
in the evening
in the afternoon
at three o'clock
at night
at Christmas
before three o'clock
until three o'clock (kann ***by three o'clock*** heißen wenn man „bis spätestens" meint)
on my birthday
on the morning of my birthday
on February, 3rd
in December
in June
in 2008
after three o'clock
from morning to night

B. Tom was born in 1997.
His birthday is in April.
It's on April 2nd.
His friend's birthday is on the same day.
It's on a Friday this year.
On Saturday they are going to have a big party.
It's always fun to have parties at the weekend! (AmE = on the weekend), It will begin at 3 o'clock and end at 11.
They'll prepare for the party from morning to night on Friday.

Ortsangaben mit Präpositionen

A. Was ist das Gegenteil von ...

on the left	____________________
in front of the house	___________ the house
on the table	____________________
into the room	___________ the room
over the house	___________ the house
near the station	far _________ the station

B. Setze die folgenden Präpositionen ein. Manche kannst du mehrmals verwenden.

at on above in in front of under next to behind

Let's have a look _______ Tom's room. _________ the left there is his bed with a lamp _______ it. ______ the right there is a wardrobe. __________ the middle of the room there is a table and some chairs. There is one window _______ his room. ________ the window (vor) there is a desk with his schoolbooks _________ it. There is a computer __________ his desk, too. There are posters ______ the wall. But Tom's room is a mess. His socks are _________ his bed (unter) and his pullover is _____ the floor, too. There is an empty bottle of Coke _____ one corner of the room and there are many CDs _______ his bed (auf). Look! And what's that ________ the computer (hinter)? There is an old sandwich ____________ an empty bag of chips (neben)!

Lösung

A. on the right
behind the house
under the table
out of the room
under the house
far from the station

B. Let's have a look at Tom's room. On the left there is his bed with a lamp above it. On the right there is a wardrobe. In the middle of the room ... There is one window in his room. In front of the window there is a desk with his schoolbooks on it. There is a computer on his desk, too. There are posters on the wall ... His socks are under his bed and his pullover is on the floor, too. There is an empty bottle of Coke in one corner of the room and there are many CDs on his bed. Look! And what's that behind the computer? There is an old sandwich next to an empty bag of chips.

Das Possessivpronomen

A. Ersetze die Substantive mit dem Possessivbegleiter durch das entsprechende Pronomen.

This is **my pen**.	It's ______________________.
Is this **your pen**?	Is it ______________________?
That's **her bag**.	That's ______________________.
That's **his book**.	That's ______________________.
This is **our dog**.	It's ______________________.
Is this **your car**?	Is this ______________________?
Are these **their bikes**?	Are these ______________________?

B. Ergänze die Possessivpronomen.

a Look at these shoes! I don't think they are ________; they aren't my size. But, perhaps they are ________, Tom. They really look as if they could be ________. No, they aren't. I never forget my trainers. I always keep ________ in my locker.

b Debbie, look here. Isn't Alice missing a blouse? Couldn't that be hers? I don't really think that blouse is ________. It's too small.

c Oh look, Betty. Aren't Sue and Mary looking for their English books? The books over there could be ______________. Let's see if we find their names in them. Oh no, they aren't ____________. They're ours!

Lösung

A. mine
yours
hers
his
ours
yours
theirs

B. a ... they aren't mine. ... perhaps they are yours, Tom. ... as if they could be yours. ... I always keep mine in my locker.
b ... that blouse is hers.
c ... could be theirs. ... they aren't theirs.

Steigerungsformen

A. Ergänze die fehlenden Formen.

Grundform	Komparativ	Superlativ
quickly	______________	______________
angrily	______________	______________
slowly	______________	______________
quietly	______________	______________
nervously	______________	______________
carefully	______________	______________
dangerously	______________	______________
terribly	______________	______________
politely	______________	______________

B. Ergänze die fehlenden Formen.

Grundform	Komparativ	Superlativ
hard	______________	______________
fast	______________	______________
well	______________	______________
badly	______________	______________
much (= sehr)	______________	______________

Lösung

A. quickly, more quickly, most quickly
angrily, more angrily, most angrily
slowly, more slowly, most slowly
quietly, more quietly, most quietly
nervously, more nervously, most nervously
carefully, more carefully, most carefully
dangerously, more dangerously, most dangerously
terribly, more terribly, most terribly
politely, more politely, most politely

B. hard, harder, hardest
fast, faster, fastest
well, better, best
badly, worse, worst
much, more, most

Adjektiv oder Adverb?

A. Ergänze die Lücken.

1. Adjektive beziehen sich immer auf ein ________________ oder ____________. Vor einem ______________ steht daher nie ein Adverb.
2. Adverbien der Art und Weise geben an, wie etwas getan wird. Sie beziehen sich daher immer auf ein ______________.
3. Ist das Verb ***to be***, steht immer ein ________________. Dies gilt jedoch nicht für die ***progressive forms*** (He is driving carefully).

B. Adjektiv oder Adverb? Setze die richtigen Formen ein.

Tom was lying ___________ (quiet) in his bed when ___________ (sudden) the door bell rang. Who could it be at that time? It was already rather ___________ (late) and he was ___________ (alone) in the house. Was he ___________ (afraid)? No, he wasn't. He ___________ (quick) got up and opened the door. Outside it was ___________ (dark) and ___________ (cold). He looked around ___________ (careful), but he couldn't see anybody. He ___________ (slow) went back to his room and to bed again. A minute later he heard the bell again. ___________ (angry) he ran down to open the door, but he couldn't see anybody again. There was only a ___________ (small) noise near the garden wall. Was somebody playing a ___________ (dirty) trick on him?

Lösung

A. 1 ein Substantiv oder ein Pronomen/Substantiv
2 Verb
3 Adjektiv

B. quietly/suddenly/late/alone/afraid/
quickly/dark and cold/carefully/slowly/
Angrily/small/dirty

Konjunktionen

A. Lies diese Geschichte und unterstreiche die Konjunktionen, die du in diesem Text findest.

A man and his dog are walking along a road. Suddenly the man remembers that he and his dog are already dead. He stops for a moment, but then walks on. After some time they come to a high, white wall. When they get near it, they see a big door in the wall and realize that the street which leads into it is made of pure gold. Then they see a man who is standing there. When they get near enough, they ask him where they are. The man tells them that this place is called heaven.

B. a Was bedeuten diese Konjunktionen auf Deutsch?

and	__________	if	__________ / __________
or	__________	when	__________
but	__________	that	__________
so	__________	so that	__________
		because	__________
		although	__________
		before	__________
		until	__________

b Was verbinden Konjunktionen wie *and*? Was verbinden Konjunktionen wie *if*?

____

Lösung

A. A man <u>and</u> his dog are walking along a road. Suddenly the man remembers <u>that</u> he <u>and</u> his dog are already dead. He stops for a moment, <u>but</u> then he walks on. After some time they come to a high, white wall. <u>When</u> they get near it, they see a big door in the wall <u>and</u> realize <u>that</u> the street which leads into it is made of pure gold. Then they see a man who is standing there. <u>When</u> they get near enough, they ask him where they are. The man tells them <u>that</u> this place is called heaven.

B. **a** ***and*** = und; ***or*** = oder; ***but*** = aber; ***so*** = so; ***if*** = wenn, falls/ob; ***when*** = wenn; ***that*** = dass; ***so that*** = so dass; ***because*** = weil; ***although*** = obwohl; ***before*** = bevor; ***until*** = bis

b Konjunktionen wie ***and, or, but, so*** verbinden gleiche Satzteile (z. B. zwei Substantive) oder gleiche Satzarten (z. B. zwei Hauptsätze), Konjunktionen wie ***if, when*** dagegen verbinden Hauptsätze mit Nebensätzen.

Mengenangaben mit *much*, *many*, *a lot of*, *lots of*

A. a Setze *much* oder *many* vor die folgenden Substantive.

________ food	________ people	________ water
________ wood	________ stories	________ countries
________ families	________ children	________ women
________ sugar	________ information	________ lemonade
________ years	________ tea	________ milk
________ courage*	________ pictures	________ coffee

* courage = Mut

b Erkläre, weshalb du bei einigen Substantiven *much*, bei anderen *many* eingesetzt hast.

____

____

B. Setze *much* / *many* / *a lot of* / *lots of* richtig ein.

How ____________ is this bike? It costs too ____________ money!

How ____________ bikes have you got here?

How ____________ bikes can you repair in a day?

How ____________ money does it cost to repair a bike?

Are there any girls in the club, too? How ____________ girls are in your club?

How ____________ time do spend there? I spend so ____________ time there!

Lösung

A. **a**

much food	much information
much wood	much tea
many families	many pictures
much sugar	much water
many years	many countries
much courage	many women
many people	much lemonade
many stories	much milk
many children	much coffee

b *Many* steht bei Substantiven im Plural (zählbare Substantive z. B. *children*); *much* bei Substantiven, die im Englischen keinen Plural haben oder haben können (unzählbare Substantive z. B. *information*).

B. How much is this bike? It costs too much money! How many bikes have you got here?
How many bikes can you repair ...?
How much money does it cost ...?
How many girls ...?
How much time ...? I spend so much time there!

Mengenangaben mit *a little, little, a few, few*

A. Übersetze die hervorgehobenen Begleiter.

I've got very **little** time today. ______________________

But I can find **a little** time for you. ______________________

I've got **a few** things to tell you. ______________________

Very **few** people know about this! ______________________

B. Vervollständige folgende Sätze.

Vor welchen Substantiven musst du **a little/little** und vor welchen Substantiven musst du **a few/few** gebrauchen?

a little/little steht vor Substantiven, die ______________________

a few/few steht vor Substantiven, die ______________________

Und was bedeutet **little** vor einem Substantiv, das einen Plural haben kann wie zum Beispiel *girl*:

She's my little girl ______________________

Handelt es sich hier auch um eine Mengenangabe? ☐ Ja ☐ Nein

Lösung

A. wenig | ein paar/einige
ein bisschen | wenig(e)

B. ... im Englischen keinen Plural haben (unzählbar sind); einen Plural haben (zählbar sind); mein kleines Mädchen; bei *my little girl* handelt es sich natürlich nicht um eine Mengenangabe.

Große Zahlen und Jahreszahlen

A. Schreibe die folgenden Zahlen aus.

100 ______________________

200 ______________________

345 ______________________

888 ______________________

1,000 ______________________

2,000 ______________________

100,000 ______________________

1,000,000 ______________________

B. Weißt du noch, wie man Jahreszahlen liest? Es ist ganz einfach:

1492	*fourteen (hundred and) ninety-two*	**1900**	*nineteen hundred*
1648	*sixteen (hundred and) forty-eight*	**2001**	*two thousand one*

Lies und schreibe die folgenden Daten aus:

1776 ______________________

2008 ______________________

1888 ______________________

1066 ______________________

1668 ______________________

1096 ______________________

2049 ______________________

Lösung

A. a/one hundred
two hundred
three hundred and forty-five
eight hundred and eighty-eight
a/one thousand
two thousand
one hundred thousand
one million

B. seventeen hundred and seventy-six
two thousand eight
eighteen hundred and eight-eight
ten hundred and sixty-six
sixteen hundred and sixty-eight
ten hundred and ninety-six
two thousand forty-nine

Ordnungszahlen, Wochentage und Monatsnamen

A. Lies die folgenden Ordnungszahlen laut und schreibe sie aus.

1st the ____________	12th ____________
2nd the ____________	14th ____________
3rd ____________	15th ____________
4th ____________	19th ____________
5th ____________	20th ____________
8th ____________	31st ____________
9th ____________	44th ____________
11th ____________	67th ____________

B. Beantworte die Fragen.

Which is the second month of the year? ____________

What about December? Which month is it? ____________

When is Christmas in English-speaking countries? On the ________ of December.

And which is the fifth month? ____________

Which is the eighth month? ____________

And what about Tuesday? Which day of the week is it? ____________

Which is the fifth day of the week? ____________

Which is the first day of the week? ____________

Look at Tom's timetable. Which lesson is Art? ____________

And which lesson is Maths? ____________

Lösung

A. the first
the second
the third
the fourth
the fifth
the eighth
the ninth
the eleventh
the twelfth
the fourteenth
the fifteenth
the nineteenth
the twentieth
the thirty-first
the forty-fourth
the sixty-seventh

B. February
the twelfth month
twenty-fifth
May
August
the second day
Friday
Monday
the sixth lesson
the third lesson

Geburtstage, Daten und Feiertage

A. Schreibe die Geburtstage wie in dem folgenden Beispiel aus:

Tom, 12: *Tom is twelve. It's his twelfth birthday.*

His father, 39	His mother, 37	His uncle, 44
His aunt, 51	His grandma, 72	His grandpa, 78

His father ______________________________.

His mother ______________________________.

His uncle ______________________________.

His aunt ______________________________.

His grandma ______________________________.

His grandpa ______________________________.

B. Lies den Geburtstagskalender laut und schreibe ihn entsprechend aus.

Tom, 2nd April: *Tom's birthday is on the second of April.*

His father, 11th August	His grandpa, 21st March
His uncle, 13th January	His mother, 14th July
	His grandma, 19th May

His father's birthday is ______________________________.

His mother's birthday is ______________________________.

His uncle's birthday is ______________________________.

His grandpa's birthday is ______________________________.

His grandma's birthday is ______________________________.

Lösung

A. His father is thirty-nine; it's his thirty-ninth birthday.
His mother is thirty-seven; it's her thirty-seventh birthday.
His uncle is forty-four; it's his forty-fourth birthday.
His aunt is fifty-one; it's her fifty-first birthday.
His grandma is seventy-two; it's her seventy-second birthday.
His grandpa is seventy-eight; it's his seventy-eighth birthday.

B. His father's birthday is on the eleventh of August.
His mother's birthday is on the fourteenth of July.
His uncle's birthday is on the thirteenth of January.
His grandpa's birthday is on the twenty-first of March.
His grandma's birthday is on the nineteenth of May.

Bejahte und verneinte Formen von *to be*

A. Schreibe die Kurzformen in Langformen um.

Hi, I'm Danny. ____________________

I'm from Sheffield. ____________________

My parents? They're from Sheffield, too. ____________________

We're new here. ____________________

And who's that in that photo? ____________________

That's my sister. ____________________

She's ten. ____________________

B. Setze die Formen von *to be* ein. Einige Formen werden verneint.

Sorry, I __________ not Ken, I _______ Tom.

You're from Bristol, right? We ___________ from Bristol, we _______ from York.

______ you new here? Yes, we __________.

_____ the girl over there your sister? No, she _______. She _________ my sister.

_______ she in your class? No, she ____________ in my class. She _______ in my sister's class.

What about the boys over there? ______ they in your class? They _________ in my class either.

And the man over there? He _______ our teacher. He ________ our caretaker.

Lösung

A. I am Danny.
I am from Sheffield.
They are from Sheffield, too.
We are new here.
And who is that in that photo?
That is my sister.
She is ten.

B. Sorry, I am not Ken, I am Tom.
... We aren't from Bristol. We are from York.
Are you new here? Yes, we are.
Is the girl over there your sister? No, she isn't. She isn't my sister.
Is Tanya in your class? No, she isn't in my class. She is in my sister's class.
... Are they in your class? No, they aren't in my class either.
... He is our teacher. He is our caretaker.

there is und *there are*

A. Entscheide, ob diese Sätze mit *there is* oder *there are* gebildet werden.

________________ lamps

________________ a lot of desks

________________ windows

________________ a lot of chairs

________________ a board

________________ a mirror

________________ posters in the classroom

B. Gib eine Kurzantwort, beantworte aber anschließend die Frage mit der Information in Klammern in einem ganzen Satz.

Beispiel: Is there a bed in your room? (ja, 2) Yes, there is. There are two beds in my room.

Is there a wardrobe in your room? (ja, 1) ____________________________

Are there books in your room? (nein) ____________________________

Is there a computer in your room? (ja, 1) ____________________________

Are there chairs in your room? (ja, 3) ____________________________

Is there a toilet in your room? (nein) ____________________________

Is there a lamp in your room? (ja, 2) ____________________________

Is there a TV set in your room? (ja, 1) ____________________________

Lösung

A. There are lamps/There are a lot of desks/
There are windows/There are a lot of chairs/
There is a board/There is a mirror/There are posters
in the classroom.

B. Yes, there is. There is one/a wardrobe in my room.
No, there aren't. There aren't any books in my room.
Yes, there is. There is one/a computer in my room.
Yes, there are. There are three chairs in my room.
No, there isn't. There isn't a toilet/There is no toilet in my room.
Yes, there is. There are two lamps in my room.
Yes, there is. There is one/a TV set in my room.

can und *may*

A.

a Setze die entsprechenden Formen von *can* und *may* ein.

I ______________ speak English, but I ______________ speak Spanish.

____________ we see each other tomorrow, Alice? No, I ____________. I'm busy.

_______________ I smoke here, sir? No, you _________________.

______________ I do my homework here? Yes, you ______________.

b Wo liegen die Unterschiede zwischen *can* und *may*?

____

____

B. Setze die Formen von *can* und *may* ein.

____________ I ask you a question, sir?

Yes, you __________________.

____________ I leave the classroom, sir?

Okay, but first tell me why you want to leave.

I must go to the toilet, sir. _____________ I leave the classroom now?

John, just have a look at your watch. _________ you tell me the time?

Yes, I ______________. It's three minutes to twelve.

Well, John, then you certainly _________ wait another three minutes.

Oh sir, I hope I ______________.

Lösung

A. **a** I can speak English, but I can't speak Spanish.
Can we see each other tomorrow, Alice? No, I can't. I'm busy.
May I smoke here, sir? No, you may not.
May I do my homework here? Yes, you may.

b *can* bedeutet, dass man etwas tun kann oder auch (umgangsprachlich) tun darf. *May* bedeutet ebenfalls „dürfen", ist aber förmlicher als *can*.

B. May I ask you a question, sir?
Yes, you may.
May I leave the classroom, sir? ...
... I must go to the toilet, sir. May I leave the classroom now?
John, just have a look at your watch. Can you tell me the time?
Yes, I can. It's three minutes to twelve.
Well, John, then you certainly can wait another three minutes.
Oh sir, I hope I can.

Die Hilfsverben *must, needn't* und *mustn't*

A. Übersetze die folgenden Sätze und Fragen.

Muss ich kommen? ______________________________.

Du darfst nicht kommen. ______________________________.

Muss er kommen? ______________________________.

Er muss nicht kommen. ______________________________.

Er braucht nicht zu kommen. ______________________________.

B. Setze bitte die entsprechenden Hilfsverben ein.

können	nicht können	dürfen	nicht dürfen	müssen	nicht brauchen/ nicht müssen
1.	1.	1. 2.	1. 2. 3.	1.	1.

Lösung

A. Must I come?
You mustn't come.
Must he come?
He needn't come.
He needn't come.

B. können – can
nicht können – can't
dürfen – can/may
nicht dürfen – can't, may not, mustn't
müssen – must
nicht müssen, nicht brauchen – needn't

Das Partizip Präsens

A. Bilde das Partizip Präsens der folgenden Verben.

clean ______	wash ______	sing ______
laugh ______	talk ______	fight ______
drink ______	eat ______	listen ______
shout ______	knock ______	do ______
watch ______	fix ______	go ______
buy ______	play ______	say ______
cry ______	try ______	carry ______

B. Beachte die Bildung des Partizip Präsens bei den folgenden Verben.

write ______	choose ______	lose ______
come ______	ride ______	take ______
change ______	have ______	drive ______
trip ______	plan ______	put ______
sit ______	clap ______	run ______
drop ______	stop ______	swim ______
cut ______	get ______	forget ______
lie ______	die ______	tie ______

Lösung

A.

cleaning
laughing
drinking
shouting
watching
buying
crying
washing
talking
eating
knocking

fixing
playing
trying
singing
fighting
listening
doing
going
saying
carrying

B.

writing
coming
changing
tripping
sitting
dropping
cutting
lying
choosing
riding
having
planning

clapping
stopping
getting
dying
losing
taking
driving
putting
running
swimming
forgetting
tying

present progressive

A. Was machen die Kinder gerade im Pausenhof? Bilde Sätze mit den folgenden Angaben.

They/eat their sandwiches ______________________________

Many/stand together in groups ______________________________

They/talk ______________________________

Somebody/shout ______________________________

Some children/play ______________________________

Two pupils/fight ______________________________

Somebody/call a teacher ______________________________

B. Lies die Regeln und fülle die Lücken aus.

a Das *present progressive* besteht immer aus zwei Teilen:

(1) aus einer Form von *to be* und (2) aus dem *Partizip Präsens*.

Shh! Be quiet! We __________ (to be) ________________ (listen) to the teacher!

b Das Partizip des Präsens bildest du, indem du *-ing* an den Infinitiv ohne *to* anhängst:

to go = ___________, to do = ___________, to try = ___________

c Bei vielen einsilbigen Verben, die auf einen Konsonant enden, wird der Konsonant verdoppelt. Bei Verben wie *to take*, die auf ein *-e* enden, das nicht ausgesprochen wird, entfällt das *-e*. Bei Verben, die wie *to lie* auf *-ie* enden, wird das *-ie* zu *-y*:

to stop = ___________, to take = ___________, to die = ___________

Lösung

A. They are eating their sandwiches.
They are standing together in groups.
They are talking.
Somebody is shouting.
Some children are playing.
Two pupils are fighting.
Somebody is calling a teacher.

B. **a** Shh! Be quiet! We are listening to the teacher!
b going, doing, trying
c stopping, taking, dying.

simple present

A. **a** Setze die dritte Person Singular ein.

he	______________	(play)	she	______________	(do)
he	______________	(carry)	she	______________	(watch)
she	______________	(go)	he	______________	(die)
he	______________	(say)	she	______________	(kiss)
he	______________	(try)	she	______________	(have)
he	______________	(buy)	she	______________	(make)

b Unterstreiche die Verben, die unregelmäßig sind und schreibe sie heraus.

______________________ ______________________

______________________ ______________________

B. Setze die 3. Person Singular ein.

His mother ____________ him up at seven. (wake)

He ____________ to wake up. (try)

He ______________, then he ______________. (wash/get dressed)

After that he _________ breakfast. (have)

He ________ goodbye to his mother. (say)

Then he _________ his things and _________ the house. (pack/leave)

He _________ to the bus station and _________ the bus. (go/catch)

Sometimes he _________ his homework on the bus. (do)

At half past eight he _______ at school. (arrive)

Lösung

A. **a** plays, carries, goes, says, tries, buys, does, watches, dies, kisses, has, makes

b to do, to go, to have, to say (nur in der Aussprache)

B. His mother wakes him up at seven.
He tries to wake up.
He washes, then he gets dressed.
After that he has breakfast.
He says goodbye to his mother.
Then he packs his things and leaves the house.
He goes to the bus station and catches the bus.
Sometimes he does his homework on the bus.
At half past eight he arrives at school.

Fragen mit Fragewörtern im *simple present*

Stelle Fragen nach den hervorgehobenen Satzteilen.

a **Mr Mason** is a teacher.

b Mr Mason is **at home**.

c He **corrects** his pupils' tests at home.

d He always corrects them **on Saturday afternoon**.

e He often finds **a lot of mistakes** in their tests.

f He doesn't always like **what he sees**.

g Sometimes **he** gets angry.

a ____ ?

b ____ ?

c ____ ?

d ____ ?

e ____ ?

f ____ ?

g ____ ?

Lösung

a Who is Mr Mason?
b Where is Mr Mason?
c What is he doing?
d When does he correct them?
e What does he often find in their tests?
f What doesn't he always like?
g Who gets angry sometimes?

simple present oder *present progressive*?

A. Das *simple present* oder das *present progressive*? Was ist richtig?

Where is David?

He ______________________ (clean) Debbie's bike.

What? Why ________ he _____________ (clean) her bike during my English lesson?

That ___________ (be) his birthday present to her.

Okay, okay, I ___________ (see). He ____________ (know) we have English today, doesn't he?

I _____________________ (think) so.

Well, maybe he _____________________ (not know) that it's my birthday, too. He can clean my car too – as a birthday present to me!

B. Das *simple present* oder das *present progressive*? Beantworte die Fragen.

a Doesn't Mr Brown live here? No, he doesn't. He ____________ in London now. (live)

b Can I talk to Debbie? I'm afraid not*. She ____________________ a bath. (have)

c Can you talk to me, Bob? Sorry, not now, I __________________ the football match on TV. (watch)

d Look! That's Bobby's team. They ________________ against another school. (play) _________ you _______ football, too? (play)

* I'm afraid not. = Leider nicht.

Lösung

A. ... He is cleaning Debbie's bike.
What? Why is he cleaning her bike during my English lesson?
That is his birthday present to her.
Okay, okay, I see. He knows we have English today, doesn't he?
I think so.
Well, maybe he doesn't know that ...

B.
- **a** He lives in London now.
- **b** She is having a bath.
- **c** I'm watching the football match on TV.
- **d** They are playing against another school. Do you play football, too?

simple past von *to be*

A. Setze die Formen des *simple past* von *to be* ein.

a Last week Tom ____________ ill.

b He ____________ at home.

c His parents ____________ also at home.

d His friends ____________ there, too.

e I ____________ there, too.

f The room ____________ full of people.

g There ____________ very little room in front of his bed.

h Everybody ____________ worried.

i Only Tom ____________ happy.

j He ____________ not at school, and he missed the English exam!

B. Setze die verneinten Vergangenheitsformen von *to be* ein.

Tom ______________ well.

His friends ______________ happy.

You ______________ happy.

His mother ______________ happy either.

His parents called the doctor, but he ______________ there.

He ______________ at home.

We ______________ happy about that.

Lösung

A. **a** Last week Tom was ill.
b He was at home.
c His parents were also at home.
d His friends were there, too.
e I was there, too.
f The room was full of people.
g There was very little room in front of his bed.
h Everybody was worried.
i Only Tom was happy.
j He was not at school ...

B. Tom wasn't well.
His friends weren't happy.
You weren't happy.
His mother wasn't happy either.
His parents called the doctor, but he wasn't there.
He wasn't at home.
We weren't happy about that.

past progressive

A. a Wie wird das *present progressive* gebildet?

Mit dem ☐ Präsens von ***to be*** ☐ Präsens von ***to do***

und dem ☐ Partizip Präsens ☐ Partizip Perfekt

b Und wie steht es mit dem *past progressive*? Es wird gebildet

mit der ☐ Vergangenheit von ***to be*** ☐ Vergangenheit von ***to do***

und dem ☐ Partizip Perfekt ☐ Partizip Präsens

c Vervollständige die folgenden Sätze:

What _______ you _________ (do) right now?

What _______ you _________ (do) yesterday when I called you?

B. Bilde Sätze mit dem *past progressive*.

When the doorbell rang yesterday morning at seven o'clock, ...

I/just get up ______________________________

my parents/have breakfast ______________________________

my father/read morning paper ______________________________

my sister/still sleep ______________________________

our neighbors/still lie in their beds ______________________________

my younger brother/still dream ______________________________

other people/have a good time ______________________________

Lösung

A. **a** Mit dem Präsens von **to be** und dem Partizip Präsens
b mit der Vergangenheit von **to be** und dem Partizip Präsens
c What are you doing right now? What were you doing yesterday when I called you?

B. When the doorbell rang yesterday at seven o'clock ...
I was just getting up.
my parents were having breakfast.
my father was reading the morning paper.
my sister was still sleeping.
our neighbors were still lying in their beds.
my younger brother was still dreaming.
other people were having a good time.

Regelmäßige und unregelmäßige Verben im *simple past*

A.

1. Bei Verben, die das *simple past* regelmäßig bilden, wird ein ________ an den Infinitiv angehängt. Wo bereits ein *-e* vorhanden ist, entfällt dieses (z. B.: *dance* + *ed* = *danced*).
2. Die Endung *-ed* wird bei Verben, die auf ein gesprochenes /t/ oder /d/ enden, wie ________ ausgesprochen (z. B. *hate* + *ed* = *hated*).
3. Ein *-y* wird nach ____________ zu *ie*; nach __________ bleibt es erhalten (z. B. *try* → *tried*, aber *play* → *played*).
4. Der letzte Konsonant bei einsilbigen Verben mit kurzem betonten Vokal wird ________________ (z. B. *drop* → *dropped*).

B. Bilde das *simple past* der folgenden Verben.

choose	____________	eat	____________	speak	____________
come	____________	fly	____________	stand	____________
do	____________	fall	____________	take	____________
drive	____________	feel	____________	tell	____________
keep	____________	leave	____________	throw	____________
lose	____________	make	____________	know	____________
meet	____________	read	____________	write	____________
have	____________	go	____________	wear	____________
hear	____________	give	____________	fight	____________
hurt	____________	hide	____________	mean	____________
sell	____________	ride	____________	find	____________

Lösung

A.
1 ... wird ein *-ed* angehängt.
2 ... wie /id/ ausgesprochen.
3 ... nach Konsonant zu *ie*, nach Vokal bleibt es erhalten.
4 ... wird verdoppelt.

B.
chose
came
did
drove
kept
lost
met
had
heard
hurt
sold
ate
flew
fell
felt
left
made

read
went
gave
hid
rode
spoke
stood
took
told
threw
knew
wrote
wore
fought
meant
found

Fragen und Antworten im *simple past*

A. Stelle die Fragen der Polizisten.

a You call us half an hour ago? ______________________________?

b You leave the window open? ______________________________?

c Anybody know that you were out tonight? ______________________________?

d You turn the lights on? ______________________________?

e You notice anything out of the ordinary*? ______________________________?

f Your neighbour notice** anything? ______________________________?

g You be out all evening? ______________________________?

h You shut that door? ______________________________?

i The burglar*** steal anything? ______________________________?

j He open that safe? ______________________________?

* anything out of the ordinary = irgendwas Außergewöhnliches

** to notice = erkennen, mitbekommen

*** burglar = Einbrecher, Dieb

B. Schaue dir die Fragen in der vorigen Aufgabe noch einmal an. Gib dann die entsprechenden Kurzantworten.

a Yes, ____________________.

b No, ____________________.

c No, nobody ____________________.

d Yes, ____________________.

e Yes, ____________________.

f No, ____________________.

g Yes, ____________________.

h No, ____________________.

i Yes, ____________________.

j Yes, ____________________.

Lösung

A.
- **a** Did you call us ...?
- **b** Did you leave the window open?
- **c** Did anybody know ...?
- **d** Did you turn the lights on?
- **e** Did you notice anything ...?
- **f** Did your neighbour notice anything?
- **g** Were you out all evening?
- **h** Did you shut that door?
- **i** Did the burglar steal anything?
- **j** Did he open that safe?

B.
- **a** Yes, we did.
- **b** No, we didn't.
- **c** No, nobody did.
- **d** Yes, we did.
- **e** Yes, we did.
- **f** No, he/she didn't.
- **g** Yes, we were.
- **h** No, we didn't.
- **i** Yes, he did.
- **j** Yes, he did.

simple past oder *past progressive*?

A. Setze die richtigen Verbformen ein.

All the children ____________ to see the young	want
polar bear, but Mr Winterbottom ____________	tell
them that the bear ____________ still too young to	be
leave its cage. So they ____________ over to see	go
the monkeys. When they ____________ there, feed-	get
ing-time _______ over. But some of the monkeys	be
__________ still very hungry. They ____________	be/eat
their bananas or _________ on their carrots and	nibble*
apples. Others ____________ so hungry any-	not be
more. Some ________ ________________ in a	sit
corner. Others _______________ somewhere in	hide
their cage and some ____________________.	sleep
Two gorillas ________________ each other. A	chase
young one ________________ near the window	stand
of his cage and _______________ at the visitors.	look

to nibble = (an)knabbern

B. Finde Beispiele für die folgenden Erklärungen in dem obigen Text.

1. Hast du das System kapiert? Du gebrauchst das *simple past* für Handlungen, die neu einsetzen, sich wiederholen oder – wie in einer Geschichte – aufeinander folgen.

   ____

2. Das *past progressive* gebrauchst du dagegen für Handlungen, die zu einem bestimmten Zeitpunkt der Vergangenheit noch nicht vorüber sind, sondern gerade ablaufen.

   ____

Lösung

A. All the children wanted to see the young polar bear, but Mr Winterbottom told them that the bear was still too young to leave its cage. So they went over to see the monkeys. When they got there, feeding-time was over. But some of the monkeys were still very hungry. They were eating their bananas or nibbling on their carrots and apples. Others were not so hungry anymore. Some were sitting in a corner. Others were hiding somewhere in their cage, and some were sleeping. Two gorillas were chasing each other. A young one was standing near the window of his cage and looking at the visitors.

B.
1 So they went over to ther monkeys' house. When they got there ...
2 They were eating their bananas, nibbling on their carrots, etc. Alles geschieht in dem Augenblick, wo die Kinder sie sehen

can, may, must, need

A. Gib Kurzantworten auf die Fragen, die seine Klassenkameraden ihm stellen.

Did you have to stay in hospital?	No, ________________
Did you have to stay in bed?	Yes, ________________
Did you have to take any medicine?	Yes, ________________
Were you allowed to watch TV?	Yes, ________________
Did you have to do any homework?	No, ________________
Were you allowed to call your friends?	Yes, ________________
Could you talk to them on the phone?	Yes, ________________
Were your friends allowed to visit you?	Yes, ________________

B. Stelle einem Freund von dir die Fragen. Gebrauche die Hilfsverben.

The last time you were ill ...

________________________ go to hospital? (Musstest du)

__________________________ stay in bed? (Wie lange musstest du)

_____________________________ see you? (Wie oft musste der Arzt)

____________ get out of bed on your own*? (Konntest du)

________________________ do in hospital? (Was durftest du nicht)

____________________ do any homework? (Musstest du)

____________ your friends ______ visit you? (Wie oft durften)

__________________________ to go home? (Wann durftest)

* on your own = alleine, ohne Hilfe von anderen

Lösung

A. No, I didn't.
Yes, I did.
Yes, I did.
Yes, I was.
No, I didn't.
Yes, I was.
Yes, I could.
Yes, they were.

B. Did you have to go to hospital?
How long did you have to stay in bed?
How often did the doctor have to see you?
Could you get out of bed on your own?
What weren't you allowed to do in hospital?
Did you have to do any homework?
How often were your friends allowed to visit you?
When were you allowed to go home?

shall und *should*

A. Mache Vorschläge mit *shall*.

buy a sandwich for you / do it for you / keep you company / carry it for you / find a place for you to sleep / explain it to you

"My schoolbag is so heavy." ____________________

"I'm so tired." ____________________

"I'm so hungry." ____________________

"I can't do my homework." ____________________

"This exercise is so difficult." ____________________

"I am so lonely." ____________________

B. Gib Ratschläge mit *should (= sollte)*. Welche Sätze passen zusammen?

a	"I'm so tired."	not eat so much
b	"My tests are so bad."	study* harder
c	"TV is boring."	ask her out on a date
d	"My jeans don't fit anymore."	look for them
e	"I'm getting so fat."	not stay up so late
f	"My skirt is so dirty."	go home now
g	"My room is a real mess."	wash it
h	"I've lost my keys."	tidy it up
i	"Alice likes me."	not watch so much TV
j	"My parents are waiting for me."	buy new ones

* to study = studieren, lernen/pauken

Lösung

A. Shall I carry it for you?
Shall I find a place for you to sleep?
Shall I buy a sandwich for you?
Shall I do it for you?
Shall I explain it to you?
Shall I keep you company?

B.
a You shouldn't stay up so late.
b You should study harder.
c You shouldn't watch so much TV.
d You should buy new ones.
e You shouldn't eat so much.
f You should wash it.
g You should tidy it up.
h You should look for them.
i You should ask her out on a date.
j You should go home now.

Ausdrücke mit *to have*

A. Ordne die Ausdrücke mit *to have* den deutschen Bedeutungen zu.

to have an accident	ein Kind haben, ein Kind bekommen
to have fun	einen Tag frei haben
to have a bath	Spaß haben, sich amüsieren
to have breakfast	Mittag essen
to have a day off	plaudern, Schwätzen halten
to have lunch	eine Pause machen
to have a chat	einen Unfall haben
to have a break	ein Bad nehmen, baden
to have a baby	frühstücken
to have a shower	duschen
to have an argument	(sich) streiten

B. Dann setze die entsprechenden Wendungen sinngemäß ein.

a It's twelve o'clock. Let's ______________________________.

b Oh dear, you smell bad! Go to the bathroom and ______________.

c My aunt is pregnant*. She will __________________ a baby soon.

d Be careful when you ride your bike! Don't __________________.

e You're going skiing this weekend? ______________! Break a leg!

* pregnant = schwanger

Lösung

A. to have an accident = einen Unfall haben
to have fun = Spaß haben, sich amüsieren
to have a bath = ein Bad nehmen, sich baden
to have breakfast = frühstücken
to have a day off = einen freien Tag haben
to have lunch = Mittag essen
to have a chat = plaudern, Schwätzchen halten
to have a break = eine Pause machen
to have a baby = ein Kind haben, ein Kind bekommen
to have a shower = sich duschen
to have an argument = streiten

B. **a** Let's have lunch.
b ... and have a bath / shower.
c She will have a baby soon.
d Don't have an accident.
e Have fun!

past participle

A. Wie du weißt, wird das *present perfect* mit den Formen von *have* und dem Partizip der Vergangenheit gebildet. Die Formen von *have* kennst du, aber weißt du auch noch, wie das Partizip gebildet wird? Bilde das *past participle* von den folgenden Verben:

talk	______	dance	______
end	______	play	______
try	______	return	______
carry	______	kill	______
drop	______	stop	______
look	______	die	______
tie	______	paint	______

Erinnern dich diese Formen an etwas? Richtig: Sie werden genauso gebildet wie die regelmäßigen Formen des ______________.

B. Wie heißt der Infinitiv der folgenden Verbformen? Achte auf die Schreibung!

chosen	______	lost	______	bought	______
meant	______	written	______	fed	______
held	______	fled	______	worn	______
felt	______	drawn	______	met	______
woken	______	given	______	told	______
sold	______	left	______	flown	______
found	______	shaken	______	hidden	______
bled	______	shown	______	broken	______

Lösung

A.

talked
ended
tried
carried
dropped
looked
tied
danced
played
returned
killed
stopped
died
painted

Sie werden genauso gebildet wie die regelmäßigen Formen des *simple past*.

B.

choose
mean
hold
feel
wake
sell
find
bleed
lose
write
flee
draw
give
leave
shake
show
buy
feed
wear
meet
tell
fly
hide
break

present perfect

A. Bilde Sätze im *present perfect* mit den folgenden Angaben.

Tom/be/to school. ______________________

He/just/come back. ______________________

His mum/be/shopping. ______________________

She/buy a lot of things. ______________________

She/do/the cooking. ______________________

She/clean the bathroom. ______________________

Tom/help her. ______________________

They/have a busy day. ______________________

They/do/a lot of things. ______________________

B. **a** Bilde Sätze im *present perfect*.

Tom's father/be/very busy, too. ______________________

He/leave the house. ______________________

But he/not be in his office. ______________________

He/not help his wife. ______________________

He/be away on business. ______________________

He/take the train to London. ______________________

b Wo stehen im *present perfect* die Ergänzungen zum Verb?

☐ vor dem Partizip ☐ hinter dem Partizip

Lösung

A. Tom has been to school.
He has just come back.
His mum has been shopping.
She has bought a lot of things.
She has done the cooking.
She has cleaned the bathroom.
Tom has helped her.
They have had a busy day.
They have done a lot of things.

B. **a** Tom's father has been very busy, too.
He has left the house.
But he has not been in his office.
He has not helped his wife.
He has been away on business.
He has taken the train to London.
b Sie stehen immer hinter dem Partizip.

present perfect oder *simple past*?

A. Das *present perfect* oder das *simple past*?

While they ________ (be) on their way to Wales, a heavy storm ________________ (hit) the area.

Luckily, they _________ (be) in their car, but they _________ (have) to stop under a bridge.

"Dear me," Mrs Benson __________ (say) to her husband, "I _____________ ______________ (never see) such a storm in all my life."

"We are lucky that we _____________________ (not have) an accident."

Luckily, after an hour or so, they _________________ (can) continue.

When they finally ___________________ (arrive) at their hotel, it _____________ (be) sunny again.

B. a Übersetze diesen Text. Pass auf, welche Zeit du nehmen musst.

Gestern sind wir um 8 Uhr abends angekommen. Wir haben unsere Koffer aus dem Wagen geholt und sind in das Hotel gegangen. Dort haben sie uns unsere Zimmer gezeigt. Wir haben dann ausgepackt. Danach haben wir ein Restaurant gesucht. Wir waren sehr hungrig.

____

____

____

b Welche Zeit ist richtig und warum?

____

Lösung

A. While they were on their way to Wales, a heavy storm hit the area. Luckily, they were in their car, but they had to stop under a bridge. "Dear me," Mrs Benson said to her husband, "I have never seen such a storm in all my life." We are lucky that we haven't had an accident." Luckily, after an hour or so, they could continue. When they finally arrived at their hotel, it was sunny again.

B.
- **a** We arrived at 8 yesterday evening. We took our bags out of our car and went into the hotel. They showed us our rooms there. Then we unpacked our things. After that we looked for a restaurant. We were very hungry.
- **b** Du musst das *simple past* gebrauchen.
  Bei den obigen Sätzen handelt es sich um aufeinanderfolgende Handlungen.

will-future

A. Setze die Sätze in das *will-future*.

The Bensons/go for a walk. ____________________

They/visit the old town. ____________________

They/go down to the harbour. ____________________

They/have a look at the boats. ____________________

They/have lunch at a restaurant. ____________________

Tom/send a text message* to a friend. ____________________

Mr Benson/buy a newspaper. ____________________

* text message = SMS (to text someone = jemandem eine SMS schreiben)

B. Setze die folgenden Sätze in das *will-future*. Gebrauche die Langformen für Satz 1 bis 4, ab Satz 5 die Kurzformen.

1. They ____________________ (not get) up early.
2. They ____________________ (not stay) hungry all day.
3. Mrs Benson ____________________ (not prepare) any sandwiches.
4. They ____________________ (not eat) sandwiches.
5. They ____________________ (not go) to the same restaurant again.
6. They ____________________ (not have) lunch there.
7. Mrs Benson ____________________ (not do) any cooking.
8. She ____________________ (not stand) in the kitchen all day.
9. She ____________________ (not be) unhappy about it.

Lösung

A. The Benson will go for a walk.
They will visit the old town.
The will go down to the harbour.
They will have a look at the boats.
They will have lunch at a restaurant.
Tom will send a text message to a friend.
Mr Benson will buy a newspaper.

B.
1 They will not get up early.
2 They will not stay hungry all day.
3 Mrs Benson will not prepare any sandwiches.
4 They will not eat sandwiches.
5 They won't go to the same restaurant again.
6 They won't have lunch there.
7 Mrs Benson won't do any cooking.
8 She won't stand in the kitchen all day.
9 She won't be unhappy about it.

Gebrauch des *going to-future*

A. Das Schuljahr beginnt bald wieder. Manche Kinder haben für das neue Schuljahr gute Vorsätze gefasst. Hier sind sie. Mache ganze Sätze daraus.

Tom / not sleep so much	Debbie / work harder
Mike and Ken / not talk so much	Fiona and Sue / not be late to class anymore
Ian / do his homework	Alice / not forget her homework
Kevin / leave the girls alone	John / not drive his teachers crazy

______________________ ______________________

______________________ ______________________

______________________ ______________________

______________________ ______________________

B. Ergänze, was fehlt.

1. What are you going to do, Tom? Are you going to work more?

   No, I ____________, but ____________________ so much.

2. And what about you, Mike? Are you going to talk less?

   Yes, ____________. I'm not ____________________ so much.

3. And what about you, Fiona and Sue? Are you going to work harder?

   No, ____________, but we ______________ to class anymore.

4. And, Ian? What about you? Are you going to do your homework?

   Yes, __________. _________________________ everyday.

Lösung

A. Tom isn't going to sleep so much.
Mike and Ken aren't going to talk so much.
Ian is going to do his homework.
Kevin is going to leave the girls alone.
Debbie is going to work harder.
Fiona and Sue are not going to be late to class anymore.
Alice is not going to forget her homework.
John isn't going to drive his teachers crazy.

B.
1 No, I'm not, but I am not going to sleep so much.
2 Yes, I am. I'm not going to talk so much.
3 No, we aren't, but we are not going to be late to class anymore.
4 Yes, I am. I'm going to do my homework everyday.

going to-future oder *will-future*?

A. Das *going to-future* bezieht sich auf die Zukunft; es wird für zukünftige feste Pläne und Absichten gebraucht.

Das *will-future* wird gebraucht,

a) wenn man ausdrücken will, dass etwas unabhängig vom eigenen Wollen in der Zukunft geschieht;

b) für Hoffnungen und Vermutungen;

c) im Hauptsatz, wenn der Nebensatz eine Bedingung oder eine Annahme enthält, die sich auf die Zukunft bezieht.

1. I think he will be there, but I'm not sure.
   ☐ richtig ☐ falsch

2. We're going to be there tomorrow. I promise!
   ☐ richtig ☐ falsch

3. I don't care what he says! I am going to watch TV tonight.
   ☐ richtig ☐ falsch

B. Setze das *going to-* oder das *will-future* ein. Vergiss nicht das *to*!

a This year Debbie ____________________ be twelve.

b She ________________________ have a big party.

c She ________________________ invite all her friends.

d She is sure that her parents ____________ let her have the party.

e She hopes that all her friends ________________ come.

f She hopes that it _____________________ not rain.

g If it doesn't rain, they ____________ be able to play in the garden.

h She doesn't know yet when everyone __________________ arrive.

Lösung

A.
1 richtig
2 richtig
3 richtig

B.
a will
b is going to
c is going to
d will
e will
f will
g will
h will

question tags

A. Ergänze den richtigen *question tag*.

Debbie is a nice girl, ______________________________ ?

She has got many friends, ______________________________ ?

Many people like her, ______________________________ ?

You like her, too, ______________________________ ?

She likes Tom, ______________________________ ?

She will see him soon, ______________________________ ?

She isn't still unhappy, ______________________________ ?

You could see it, ______________________________ ?

She didn't feel well yesterday, ______________________________ ?

But she wasn't ill, ______________________________ ?

There was no need to worry, ______________________________ ?

B.

1. Handelt es sich bei Bestätigungsfragen um richtige Fragen?

   ☐ ja ☐ nein

2. Woran werden sie angehängt?

   ☐ an die Frage ☐ an den Aussagesatz

3. Sind sie positiv, wenn der vorausgehende Satz negativ ist und umgekehrt?

   ☐ ja ☐ nein

4. Gelten für ihre Bildung dieselben Regeln wie für Kurzantworten?

   ☐ ja ☐ nein

Lösung

A.

... isn't she?
... hasn't she?
... don't they?
... don't you?
... doesn't she?
... won't she?

... is she?
... couldn't you?
... did she?
... was she?
... was there?

B.

1 nein
2 an den Ausagesatz
3 ja
4 ja

Die Stellung des Subjekts

A. Übersetze die Sätze.

Heute bin ich krank.

____

Heute kann ich im Bett bleiben.

____

Heute muss ich nicht früh aufstehen.

____

Heute habe ich Fieber.

____

Wenn ich krank bin, kann ich zu Hause bleiben.

____

Heute bin ich glücklich.

____

B. Stelle Fragen.

The children are back. ____________________ ?

Two children are ill. ____________________ ?

They can't come. ____________________ ?

They caught a cold yesterday. ____________________ ?

The teachers are there, too. ____________________ ?

Lessons will begin soon. ____________________ ?

A teacher is coming. ____________________ ?

The classroom door opens. ____________________ ?

Lösung

A. Today I am ill.
Today I can stay in bed.
Today I needn't get up early.
Today I have a temperature.
When I am ill, I can stay at home.
Today I am happy.

B. Are the children back?
Are two children ill?
Can't they come?
Did they catch a cold yesterday?
Are the teachers there, too?
Will lessons begin soon?
Is a teacher coming?
Does the classroom door open?

Die Stellung des Objekts

A. **a** Übersetze die folgenden Sätze.

Hast du **Tom** gesehen?

___

Ich kann **ihn** nicht finden.

___

Ja, ich habe **ihn** gesehen.

___

Als ich ihn sah, hat er **Debbie** gesucht.

___

Er hat auch **eine CD** gesucht.

___

b Wo steht im Englischen das Objekt? Wo steht es im Deutschen?

___

___

B. Wie lauten die Sätze richtig?

I have him just seen. ___

He will to Debbie's house again go. ___

He will the house again leave. ___

He has something forgotten. ___

He must for it look. ___

Lösung

A. **a** Have you seen Tom?
I can't find him.
Yes, I have seen him.
When I saw him, he was looking for Debbie.
He was looking for a CD, too.

b Im Englischen stehen Objekte immer nach dem Verb oder der Verbgruppe.
Im Deutschen trennt man Hilfsverb + Verb-Konstruktionen, sodass ein Objekt immer dazwischen liegt.

B. I have just seen him.
He will go to Debbie's house again.
He will leave the house again.
He has forgotten something.
He must look for it.

Die Stellung von Orts- und Zeitangaben

A. Schreibe auf, was Tom tun will.

Monday	clean my bike	*On Monday, he's going to clean his bike.*
Tuesday	study for a test	
Wednesday	play table tennis	
Thursday	see Debbie	
Friday	practice playing the guitar	
Saturday	watch a football match on TV	
Sunday	go to the cinema with Debbie	

B. Sage, was du tun willst. Gebrauche dabei die folgenden Zeitangaben:

tonight *on Monday* *next week* *this summer*

in July *this school year*

____ (learn French)

____ (stay in bed)

____ (go to a pop concert)

____ (work more)

____ (go on holidays)

____ (go to Spain)

Lösung

A. On Tuesday he's going to study for a test.
On Wednesday he is going to play table tennis.
On Thursday, he is going to see Debbie.
On Friday, he is going to practice playing the guitar.
On Saturday he is going to watch a football match on TV.
On Sunday he is going to go to the cinema with Debbie.

B. Mögliche Lösungen:
Tonight I'm going to learn French.
On Monday I'm going to stay in bed.
Next week I'm going to go to a pop concert.
This school year I'm going to work more.
This summer I'm going to go on holidays.
In July I'm going to go to Spain.

Die Stellung der Adverbien

A. Setze die entsprechenden Adverbien der Häufigkeit ein.

They are loud (often). ______________________

They run around (always). ______________________

They have learned to sit still (never). ______________________

They listen (never). ______________________

They forget their homework (usually). ______________________

Have you met such people (ever)? ______________________

They drive their teachers crazy (sometimes). ______________________

B. Übersetze folgende Sätze.

a „Ich muss gehen", sagte er ruhig.

____

b Er machte langsam die Tür zu.

____

c Er schloss die Tür sorgfältig ab.

____

d Dann öffnete er schnell seine Tasche.

____

e Er steckte schnell den Schlüssel hinein.

____

Lösung

A. They are often loud.
They always run around.
They have never learned to sit still.
They never listen.
They usually forget their homework.
Have you ever met such people?
Sometimes they drive their teachers crazy./They sometimes drive their teachers crazy.

B.
- **a** "I have to go", he said quietly.
- **b** He slowly closed the door./He closed the door slowly.
- **c** He carefully locked the door./He locked the door carefully.
- **d** Then he quickly opened his bag./Then he opened his bag quickly.
- **e** He quickly put the key in it./He put the key in it quickly.

Die Relativpronomen *who, which, whose*

A. Definiere die hervorgehobenen Substantive. Verwende ein Relativpronomen.

a bus driver/drive a bus

Beispiel: A bus driver is somebody ______________________________.

a shopkeeper/have got a shop

____.

a shop assistant/work in a shop

____.

a customer/buy things in a shop

____.

B. Bilde Sätze mit *which* und *who*.

1. A teacher is somebody ____________________ asks a lot of questions.
2. A classmate is somebody ____________________ is in the same class.
3. School is something ____________________ is never boring.
4. A school report is something ______________ can make my parents cry.
5. A pupil is somebody ____________________ still goes to school.
6. Homework is something ____________________ can drive you crazy.
7. An English lesson is something ____________ can be fun.

Lösung

A. A bus driver is somebody who drives a bus.
A shop keeper is somebody who has got a shop.
A shop assistant is somebody who works in a shop.
A customer is somebody who buys things in a shop.

B.
1 who
2 who
3 which
4 which
5 who
6 which
7 which

Bitte hier ausfüllen

und in der nächstgelegenen Schülerhilfe vor Ort abgeben.
Weitere Infos über die Schülerhilfe unter www.schuelerhilfe.de.

Vorname

Name

PLZ

Ort

Straße

Geburtsdatum

Telefon

E-Mail

*Gültig nur in teilnehmenden Schülerhilfen. Gültig nur für Neukunden. Nur ein Gutschein pro Kunde. Nicht gültig in Verbindung mit anderen Aktionen, Angeboten, Coupons oder Rabatten. Gültig nur für Einzelunterricht in kleinen Gruppen.